THE
OFFICIAL FAIR-USE
GUIDELINES

Fourth Edition

COPYRIGHT INFORMATION SERVICES

The federal documents contained in this booklet are in the public dom∎ The editorial notes and the organization and arrangement of the booklet are subject to copyright protection. The "1987 Statement on Software Copyright: ∤ ICCE Policy Statement" is reproduced by permission of the Software Copyrigh∎ Committee of the International Council for Computers in Education, The University of Oregon, 1787 Agate St., Eugene, OR 97403.

COPYRIGHT INFORMATION SERVICES

An imprint of the Association for Educational Communications and Technology 1025 Vermont Ave., NW, Suite 820, Washington, DC 20005. Phone: 202-347-7834; Fax: 202-347-7839.

ISBN 0-914143-21-2

The first edition of this booklet was published in 1985 under the title *Three Fair-use Guidelines: The Complete Texts Arranged for Use by Educator∎* It was replaced, four months later, by an expanded edition: *Official Fair Use Guidelines: Complete Texts of Four Official Documents Arranged for Use by Educators.* After two printings, it was replaced by the third edition, which included the ICCE Policy Statement. After several printings, the Third Edition was replaced by the Fourth Edition, which includes Congressional "Guidelines Videotaping and Captioning Television Programs for Deaf and Hearing-impair∎ Students" plus small additions and corrections to the other documents.

The Association for Educational Communications and Technology is ∎ international professional association dedicated to the improvement of instructi∎ through the effective use of media and technology. Periodicals, monographs, videotapes and audiotapes available through AECT meet the needs of media an∎ learning resource specialists, educators, librarians, industrial trainers, and a var∎ of other educational technology professionals.

TABLE OF CONTENTS

INTRODUCTION TO THE SECOND EDITION

In consulting with school districts, I frequently discover my clients ar distributing incomplete or inaccurate texts of the federal fair-use guideline teachers are expected to observe. Unfortunately, the inaccurate or truncate versions of the documents frequently distort the purpose and scope of th original documents. Those documents have been gathered in this booklet in th hope the booklet will facilitate an accurate application of the guidelines.

The first edition of this book: *Three Fair-Use Guidelines* was sold ou within a few months of its publication. At the suggestion of a client, the bookle was expanded to include the ICCE "Policy Statement on Network and Multipl Machine Software."

I hope the expanded version proves to be useful. Citations to th document sources appear on page 23.

May, 1985   Jerome K. Miller

INTRODUCTION TO THE THIRD EDITION

This booklet has proven to be very popular with educators. So popula in fact, that it is our best selling publication. I hope the third edition, whic includes the new ICCE Policy, continues to be useful to educators. I occasional hear rumors about additional fair use guidelines being written. If a substantiv copyright policy or fair-use guideline is issued by Congress or a profession association, this edition will be replaced by a fourth edition containing the ne document. Readers are urged to suggest additional documents to be include in future editions.

April, 1987   Jerome K. Miller

INTRODUCTION TO THE FOURTH EDITION

This edition has been expanded, at a client's suggestion, to include th Congressional Record explanation of fair use copying of television program and captioning those programs for deaf and hearing-impaired students. It als includes one correction to the music guidelines and supplementary documen pertaining to the guidelines for videotaping off the air.

September, 1989   Jerome K. Miller

4

I. FAIR USE GUIDELINES FOR BOOKS AND PERIODICALS

In a joint letter to Chairman Kastenmeier, dated March 19, 1976, the representatives of the Ad Hoc Committee of Educational Institutions and Organizations on Copyright Law Revision, and of the authors League of America, Inc., and the Association of American Publisher, Inc., stated:

You may remember that in our letter of March 8, 1976 we told you that the negotiating teams representing authors and publishers and the Ad Hoc Group had reached tentative agreement on guidelines to insert in the Committee Report covering educational copying from books and periodicals under Section 107 of H.R. 2223 and S. 22, and that as part of that tentative agreement each side would accept the amendments to Sections 107 and 504 which were adopted by your Subcommittee on March 3, 1976.

We are now happy to tell you that the agreement has been approved by the principals and we enclose a copy herewith. We had originally intended to translate the agreement into language suitable for inclusion in the legislative report dealing with Section 107, but we have since been advised by committee staff that this will not be necessary.

As stated above, the agreement refers only to copying from books and periodicals, and it is not intended to apply to musical or audiovisual works.

The full text of the agreement is as follows:

AGREEMENT ON GUIDELINES FOR CLASSROOM COPYING IN NOT-FOR-PROFIT EDUCATIONAL INSTITUTIONS WITH RESPECT TO BOOKS AND PERIODICALS

The purpose of the following guidelines is to state the minimum and not the maximum standards of educational fair use under Section 107 of H.R. 2223. The parties agree that the conditions determining the extent of permissible copying for educational purposes may change in the future; that certain types of copying permitted under these guidelines may not be permissible in the future; and conversely that in the future other types of copying not permitted under these guidelines may be permissible under revised guidelines.

Moreover, the following statement of guidelines is not intended to limit the types of copying permitted under the standards of fair use under judicial decision and which are stated in Section 107 of the Copyright Revision Bill There may be instances in which copying which does not fall within the guidelines stated below may nonetheless be permitted under the criteria of fair use.

GUIDELINES

I. Single Copying for Teachers

A single copy may be made of any of the following by or for a teacher at his or her individual request for his or her scholarly research or use in teaching or preparation to teach a class:

- A. A chapter from a book;

- B. An article from a periodical or newspaper;

- C. A short story, short essay or short poem, whether or not from a collective work;

- D. A chart, graph, diagram, drawing, cartoon or picture from a book, periodical, or newspaper;

II. Multiple Copies for Classroom Use

Multiple copies (not to exceed in any event more than one copy per pupil in a course) may be made by or for the teacher giving the course for classroom use or discussion; provided that:

- A. The copying meets the tests of brevity and spontaneity as defined below; and,

- B. Mets the cumulative effect test as defined below; and,

- C. Each copy includes a notice of copyright

Definitions

Brevity

(i) Poetry: (a) A complete poem if less than 250 words and if printed on not more than two pages or, (b) from a longer poem, an excerpt of not more than 250 words.

(ii) Prose: (a) Either a complete article, story or essay of less than 2,500 words, or (b) an excerpt from any prose work of not more than 1,000 words or 10% of the work, whichever is less, but in any event a minimum of 500 words.

[Each of the numerical limits stated in "i" and "ii" above may be expanded to permit the completion of an unfinished line of a poem or of an unfinished prose paragraph.]

(iii) Illustration: One chart, graph, diagram, drawing, cartoon or picture per book or per periodical issue.

(iv) "Special" works: Certain works in poetry, prose or in "poetic prose" which often combine language with illustrations and which are intended sometimes for children and at other times for a more general audience fall short of 2,500 words in their entirety. Paragraph "ii" above notwithstanding such "special works" may not be reproduced in their entirety; however, an excerpt comprising not more than two of the published pages of such special work and containing not more then 10% of the words found in the text thereof, may be reproduced.

Spontaneity

(i) The copying is at the instance and inspiration of the individual teacher, and

(ii) The inspiration and decision to use the work and the moment of its use for maximum teaching effectiveness are so close in time that it would be unreasonable to expect a timely reply to a request for permission.

Cumulative Effect

(i) The copying of the material is for only one course in the school in which the copies are made.

(ii) Not more than one short poem, article, story, essay or two excerpts may be copied from the same author, nor more than three from the same collective work or periodical volume during one class term.

(iii) There shall not be more than nine instances of such multiple copying for one course during one class term.

[The limitations stated in "ii" and "iii" above shall not apply to current news periodicals and newspapers and current news sections of other periodicals.]

III.   Prohibitions as to I and II Above

Notwithstanding any of the above, the following shall be prohibited:

(A) Copying shall not be used to create or to replace or substitute for anthologies, compilations or collective works. Such replacement or substitution may occur whether copies of various works or excerpts therefrom are accumulated or reproduced and used separately.

(B) There shall be no copying of or from works intended to be "consumable" in the course of study or of teaching. These include workbooks, exercises, standardized tests and test booklets and answer sheets and like consumable materials.

    (C)   Copying shall not:

        (a)   substitute for the purchase of books, publishers' reprints or periodicals;

        (b)   be directed by higher authority;

        (c)   be repeated with respect to the same item by the same teacher from term to term.

    (D)   No charge shall be made to the student beyond the actual cost of the photocopying.

Agreed March 19, 1976.

Ad Hoc Committee on Copyright Law Revision:

By SHELDON ELLIOTT STEINBACH.

Author-Publisher Group:

Authors League of America: By IRWIN KARP, Counsel.

Association of American Publishers, Inc.:

By ALEXANDER C. HOFFMAN, Chairman, Copyright Committee.

II. FAIR USE GUIDELINES FOR MUSIC

In a joint letter dated April 30, 1976, representatives of the Music Publishers' Association of the United States, Inc., the National Music Publishers' Association, Inc., the Music Teachers National Association, the Music Educators National Conference, the National Association of Schools of Music, and the Ad Hoc Committee on Copyright Law Revision, wrote to Chairman Kastenmeier as follows:

During the hearings on H.R. 2223 in June 1975, you and several of your subcommittee members suggested that concerned groups should work together in developing guidelines which would be helpful to clarify Section 107 of the bill.

Representatives of music educators and music publishers delayed their meetings until guidelines had been developed relative to books and periodicals. Shortly after that work was completed and those guidelines were forwarded to your subcommittee, representatives of the undersigned music organizations met together with representatives of the Ad Hoc Committee on Copyright Law Revision to draft guidelines relative to music.

We are very pleased to inform you that the discussions thus have been fruitful on the guidelines which have been developed. Since private music teachers are an important factor in music education, due consideration has been given to the concerns of that group.

We trust that this will be helpful in the report on the bill to clarify Fair Use as it applies to music.

The text of the guidelines accompanying this letter is as follows:

GUIDELINES FOR EDUCATIONAL USES OF MUSIC

The purpose of the following guidelines is to state the minimum and not the maximum standards of educational fair use under Section 107 of HR 2223. The parties agree that the conditions determining the extent of permissible copying for educational purposes may change in the future; that certain types of copying permitted under these guidelines may not be permissible in the future, the conversely that in the future other types of copying not permitted under these guidelines may be permissible under revised guidelines.

Moreover, the following statement of guidelines is not intended to limit the types of copying permitted under the standards of fair use under judicial decision and which are stated in Section 107 of the Copyright Revision Bill. There may be instances in which copying which does not fall within the guidelines stated below may nonetheless be permitted under the criteria of fair use.

A.   Permissible Uses

1. Emergency copying to replace purchased copies which for any reason are not available for an imminent performance provided purchased replacement copies shall be substituted in due course.

2. For academic purposes other than performance, single or multiple copies of excerpts of works may be made, provided that the excerpts do not comprise a part of the whole which would constitute a performable unit such as a selection, movement or aria, but in no case more than 10% of the whole work. The number of copies shall not exceed one copy per pupil.[1]

3. Printed copies which have been purchased may be edited or simplified provided that the fundamental character of the work is not distorted or the lyrics, if any, altered or lyrics added of none exist.

4. A single copy of recordings of performances by students may be made for evaluation or rehearsal purposes and may be retained by the educational institution or individual teacher.

5. A single copy of a sound recording (such as a tape, disc or cassette) of copyrighted music may be made from sound recordings owned by an educational institution or an individual teacher for the purpose of constructing aural exercises or examinations and may be retained by the educational institution or individual teacher. (This pertains only to the copyright of the music itself and not to any copyright which may exist in the sound recording.)

B. Prohibitions

1. Copying to create or replace or substitute for anthologies, compilations or collective works.

2. Copying of or from works intended to be "consumable" in the course of study or of teaching such as workbooks, exercises, standardized tests and answer sheets and like material.

3. Copying for the purpose of performance, except as in A(1) above.

4. Copying for the purpose of substituting for the purchase of music, except as in A(1) and A(2) above.

5. Copying without inclusion of the copyright notice which appears on the printed copy.

NOTES

[1] Section A-2 was revised at the last moment, at the request of the joint committee that prepared the guidelines. The original text of section 2 consisted of two parts. Part 2 (a) was redesignated in the final text as Part 2, as it appears in page 10. Part 2 (b) of the orginal text was deleted. The deleted text read:

"(b) For academic purposes other than performance, a single copy of an ntire performable unit (section, movement, aria, etc.) that is, (1) confirmed by the copyright proprietor to be out of print or (2) unavailable except in a larger ork, may be made by or for a teacher solely for the purpose of his or her holarly research or in preparation to teach a class."

III. FAIR USE GUIDELINES FOR OFF-AIR VIDEOTAPING

In March of 1979, Congressman Robert Kastenmeier, chairman of the House Subcommittee on Courts, Civil Liberties, and Administration of Justice appointed a Negotiating Committee consisting of representatives of education organizations, copyright proprietors, and creative guild and unions. The following guidelines reflect the Negotiating Committee's consensus as to the application of "fair use" to the recording, retention, and use of television broadcast programs for educational purposes. They specify periods of retention and use of such off-air recordings in classrooms and similar places devoted to instruction and for homebound instruction. The purpose of establishing these guidelines is to provide standards for both owners and users of copyrighted television programs.

GUIDELINES FOR OFF-AIR RECORDING OF BROADCAST PROGRAMMING FOR EDUCATIONAL PURPOSES

1. The guidelines were developed to apply only to off-air recording by nonprofit educational institutions.

2. A broadcast program may be recorded off-air simultaneously with broadcast transmission (including simultaneous cable retransmission) and retained by a nonprofit educational institution for a period not to exceed the first forty-five (45) consecutive calendar days after date of recording. Upon conclusion of such retention period, all off-air recordings must be erased or destroyed immediately. "Broadcast programs" are television programs transmitted by television stations for reception by the general public without charge.

3. Off-air recordings may be used once by individual teachers in the course of relevant teaching activities, and repeated once only when instructional reinforcement is necessary, in classrooms and similar places devoted to instruction within a single building, cluster or campus, as well as in the homes of students receiving formalized home instruction, during the first ten (10) consecutive school days in the forty-five (45) day calendar day retention period. "School days" are school session days—not counting weekends, holidays, vacations, examination periods, and other scheduled interruptions—within the forty-five (45) calendar day retention period.

4. Off-air recordings may be made only at the request of and used by individual teachers, and may not be regularly recorded in anticipation of

12

requests. No broadcast program may be recorded off-air more than once at the request of the same teacher, regardless of the number of times the program may be broadcast.

5. A limited number of copies may be reproduced from each off- air recording to meet the legitimate needs of teachers under these guidelines. Each such additional copy shall be subject to all provision governing the original recording.

6. After the first ten (10) consecutive school days, off-air recordings may be used up to the end of the forty-five (45) calendar day retention period only for teacher evaluation purposes i.e., to determine whether or not to include the broadcast program in the teaching curriculum, and may not be used in the recording institution for student exhibition or any other non-evaluation purpose without authorization.

7. Off-air recordings need not be used in their entirety, but the recorded programs may not be altered from their original content. Off-air recordings may not be physically or electronically combined or merged to constitute teaching anthologies or compilations.

8. All copies of off-air recording must include the copyright notice on the broadcast program as recorded.

9. Educational institutions are expected to establish appropriate control procedures to maintain the integrity of these guidelines.

CORRESPONDENCE RELATED TO THE GUIDELINES

Motion Picture Association of America, Inc.
New York, N.Y.,
August 24, 1981

Re Guidelines for Off-Air Recording of Broadcast Programming for Education Purposes.

Mr. Leonard Wasser
Writers Guild of America, East, Inc.,
New York, N.Y.

Dear Len:

This is to advise you that, although we were a party to the discussions which led to their formulation, the Motion Picture Association of America, as such will take no position on the above-style guidelines.

However, we are authorized to advise you that the following individual MPAA member companies assent to the guidelines:

Avco Embassy Pictures Corp.
Columbia Pictures Industries, Inc.
Filmways Pictures, Inc.
Metro-Goldwyn-Mayer Film Co.
Paramount Pictures Corp.
Twentieth Century-Fox Film Corp.
Universal Pictures, a division of Universal City Studios, Inc.

I would appreciate it if a copy of this letter could be included in any transmittal which you and Eileen Cooke make to Congressman Kastenmeier so that it is made part of the record.

Kindest regards.

Very truly yours,

James Bouras

Association of Media Producers
Washington, D.C.,
September 17, 1981

Ion. Robert C. Kastenmeier,Chairman,
ubcommittee on Courts, Civil Liberties and the Administration of Justice,
J.S. House of Representatives,
Vashington, D.C.

)ear Congressman Kastenmeier:

The Association of Media Producers, the national trade association
epresenting the producers and distributors of educational media matterrials,
ias appreciated the opportunity to participate as a member of the Negotiating
Committee to establish guidelines for off-air taping of copyrighted works.

This is to advise you the AMP Board of Directors recently voted not to
endorse the "Guidelines for Off-Air Recording of Broadcast Programming for
Educational Purposes," now being submitted to the Committee on Courts, Civil
Liberties and the Administration of Justice.

The guidelines are not in keeping with the principal objectives of our
ndustry, and we are fearful that they may seriously jeopardize the future
vell-being of the small but vital educational media industry, its market, and the
availability of a broad variety of instructional materials essential to maintaining
juality educational programs.

Sincerely,

Gordon L. Nelson, President

Films, Inc
Wilmette, Ill.
September 15, 198

Mr. Gordon Nelson, President,
Association of Media Producers,
1101 Connecticut Avenue,
Washington, D.C.

Dear Gordon:

As you know since approximately January 1, 1980 I have represented the Association of Media Producers on the Committee to Negotiate Fair-use Guidelines for Off-air Videotaping For Educational Uses. At that time James LeMay, formerly of Coronet Instructional Media, also represented AMP. Prior to the time I began serving on the committee Mr. Gale Livengood of Films Inc was in that capacity.

I have steadfastly recommended adoption of the guidelines to the Board of Directors of AMP and since becoming a member of the Board earlier this year, continued to take that position. I believe that adoption of the guidelines would be a positive development in the educational audio-visual industry. My recommendation to the Board also reflects the overwhelming opinion throughout my company on this issue.

As you also know, my recommendation was continually made during the actual voting by the Board on this matter but that in spite of my recommendation and vote in favor of adoption of the guidelines, the question was narrowly defeated.

I wish to have this letter become a part of the materials you transmit to Eileen Cooke of the American Library Association regarding AMP's decision You should also know that Films Inc. intends to transmit its own views on this issue directly to Congressman Robert Kastenmeier.

Sincerely yours,

Ivan R. Bender

Vice President and General Counsel

IV. GUIDELINES FOR VIDEOTAPING AND CAPTIONING TELEVISION PROGRAMS FOR DEAF AND HEARING-IMPAIRED STUDENTS

NOTE: Unlike the other documents in this booklet, this brief statement was not prepared by an outside committee, but was added by Congressman Robert Kastenmeier during the floor considerations of the Copyright Revision Act of 1976 to define legislative intent. The committee mentioned in the text is the House of Representatives Subcommittee on the Courts Civil Liberties and the Administration of Justice.

Also in consultation with section 107, the committee's attention has been directed to the unique educational needs and problems of the approximately 0,000 deaf and hearing-impaired students in the United States, and the inadequacy of both public and commercial television to serve their educational needs. It has been suggested that, as long as clear-cut constraints are imposed and enforce, the doctrine of fair use is broad enough to permit the making of an off-the-air fixation of a television program within a nonprofit educational institution for the deaf and hearing impaired, the reproduction of a master and a work copy of a captioned version of the original fixation, and the performance of the program from the work copy within the confines of the institution. In identifying the constraints that would have to be imposed within an institution in order for these activities to be considered as fair use, it has been suggested that the purpose of the use would have to be noncommercial in every respect, and educational in the sense that is serves as part of a deaf or hearing-impaired student's learning environment within the institution, and that the institution would have to insure that the master and work copy would remain in the hands of a limited number of authorized personnel within the institution, would be responsible for assuring against its unauthorized reproduction or distribution, or its performance or retention for other than educational purposes within the institution. Work copies of captioned programs could be shared among institutions for the deaf abiding by the constraints specified. Assuming that these constraints are both imposed and enforced, and that no other factors intervene to render the use unfair, the committee believes that the activities described could reasonably be considered fair use under section 107.

V. 1987 STATEMENT ON SOFTWARE COPYRIGHT: AN ICCE POLICY STATEMENT

Background

During 1982-83, educators, software developers, and hardware and software vendors cooperated to develop the *ICCE Policy Statement on Network and Multiple Machine Software*. This Policy Statement was adopted by the Board of Directors of the International Council for Computers in Education (ICCE) in 1983, and was published and distributed. It has received support from hardware and software vendors, industry associations and other education associations. One component of the Policy Statement, the "Model District Policy on Software Copyright," has been adopted by school districts throughout the world.

Now, three years later, as the educational computer market has changed and the software market has matured, ICCE has responded to suggestions that the policy statement be reviewed by a new committee and revisions be made to reflect the changes that have taken place both in the market place and in the schools.

The 1986-87 ICCE Software Copyright Committee is composed of educators, industry associations, hardware vendors, software developers and vendors, and lawyers. All the participants of this new Committee agree that the educational market should be served by developers and preserved by educators. To do so requires that the ICCE Policy Statement be revisited every few years while the industry and the use of computers in education are still developing.

Responsibilities

In the previous Policy Statement, lists of responsibilities were assigned to appropriate groups: educators; hardware vendors; and software developers and vendors. The suggestion that school boards show their responsibility by approving a district copyright policy was met with enthusiasm, and many districts approved a policy based on the ICCE Model Policy. The suggestion that software vendors adopt multiple-copy discounts and offer lab packs to schools was likewise well received; many educational software publishers now offer such pricing. It is therefore the opinion of this committee that, for the most par, the 1983 list of recommendations has become a fait accompli within the industry, and to repeat it here would be an unnecessary redundancy.

Note: The International Council for Computers in Education was recently renamed, the International Society for Technology in Education.

Nevertheless, the Committee does suggest that all parties involved in the educational computing market be aware of what the other parties are doing to reserve this market, and that the following three recommendations be considered for adoption by the appropriate agencies.

School District Copyright Policy

The Committee recommends that school districts approve a District Copyright Policy that includes both computer software and other media. A Model District Policy on Software Copyright is enclosed.

Particular attention should be directed to item five, recommending that *only one* person in the district be given the authority to sign software licensing agreements. This implies that such a person should become familiar with licensing and purchasing rights of all copyrighted materials.

Suggested Software Use Guidelines

In the absence of clear legislation, legal opinion or case law, it is suggested that school districts adopt the enclosed Suggested Software Use Guidelines as guidelines for software use within the district. The recommendation of Guidelines is similar to the situation currently used by many education agencies for off-air video recording. While these Guidelines do not carry the force of law, they do represent the collected opinion on fair software use for nonprofit education agencies from a variety of experts in the software copyright field.

Copyright Page Recommendations

The Committee recommends that educators look to the copyright page of software documentation to find their rights, obligations and license restrictions regarding an individual piece of software.

The Committee also suggests that software publishers use the documentation copyright page to *clearly* delineate the users' (owners' or licensees') rights in at least these five areas:

1. How is a back-up copy made or obtained, how many are allowed, and how are the back-ups to be used (e.g., not to be used on a second machine at the same time)?

2. Is it permissible to load the disk(s) into multiple computers for use at the same time?

3. Is it permissible to use the software on a local area network, and w‹ the company support such use? Or is a network version available from tᴾ publisher?

4. Are lab packs or quantity discounts available from the publisher?

5. Is it permissible for the owner or licensee to make copies of the printe‹ documentation? or are additional copies available, and how?

ICCE — Suggested Software Use Guidelines

The 1976 U.S. Copyright Act and its 1980 Amendments remain vague ᵢ some areas of software use and its application to education. Where the law itse‹ is vague, software licenses tend to be much more specific. It is therefoᴿ imperative that educators read the software's copyright page and understan‹ the licensing restrictions printed there. If these uses are not addressed, tᴾ following Guidelines are recommended.

These Guidelines do not have the force of law, but they do represent tᴾ collected opinion on fair software use by nonprofit educational agencies froᴍ a variety of experts in the software copyright field.

Back-up Copy: The Copyright Act is clear in permitting the owner ‹ software a back-up copy of the software to be held for use as an archival coᴘ in the event the original disk fails to function. Such back-up copies are not ‹ be used on a second computer at the same time the original is in use.

Multiple-loading: The Copyright Act is most unclear as it applies ‹ loading the contents of one disk into multiple computers for use at the samᴇ time. In the absence of a license expressly permitting the user to load tᴾ contents of one disk into many computers for use at the same time, it is suggeste‹ that you not allow this activity to take place. The fact that you physically can ‹ so is irrelevant. In an effort to make it easier for schools to buy software for eaᴄ computer station, many software publishers offer lab packs and other quantiᵗ buying incentives. Contact individual publishers for details.

Local Area Network Software Use: It is suggested that before placing software program on a local area network or disk- sharing system for use ᵇ multiple users at the same time, you obtain a written license agreement froᴍ the copyright holder giving you permission to ao so. The fact that you are abᴸ to physically load the program on the network is, again, irrelevant. You shouᴸ obtain a license permitting you to do so before you act.

Model District Policy on Software Copyright

It is the intent of [district] to adhere to the provisions of copyright laws in the area of microcomputer software. It is also the intent of the district to comply with the license agreements and/or policy statements contained in the software packages used in the district. In circumstances where the interpretation of the copyright law is ambiguous, the district shall look to the applicable license agreement to determine appropriate use of the software (or the district will abide by the approved Software Use guidelines).

We recognize that computer software piracy is a major problem for the industry and that violations of copyright laws contribute to higher costs and greater efforts to prevent copying and/or lessen incentives for the development of effective educational uses of microcomputers. Therefore, in an effort to discourage violation of copyright laws and to prevent such illegal activities:

1. The ethical and practical implications of software piracy will be taught to educators and school children in all schools in the district (e.g., covered in fifth grade social studies classes).

2. District employees will be informed that they are expected to adhere to section 117 of the 1976 Copyright Act as amended in 1980, governing the use of software (e.g., each building principle will devote one faculty meeting to the subject each year).

3. When permission is obtained from the copyright holder to use software on a disk-sharing system, efforts will be made to secure this software from copying.

4. Under no circumstances shall illegal copies of copyrighted software be made or used on school equipment.

5. [Name or job title] of this school district is designated as the only individual who may sign license agreements for software for schools in the district. Each school using licensed software should have a signed copy of the software agreement.

6. The principal at each school site is responsible for establishing practices which will enforce this district copyright policy at the school level.

The Board of Directors of the International Council for Computers in Education approved this policy statement January, 1987. The members of the 1986 ICCE Software Copyright Committee are:

Sueann Ambron, American Association of Publishers
Gary Becker, Seminole Co. Public Schools, Florida
Daniel T. Brooks, Cadwalader, Wickersham & Taft
LeRoy Finkel, International Council for Computers in Education
Virginia Helm, Western Illinois University
Kent Kehrberg, Minnesota Educational Computing Corp.
Dan Kunz, Commodore Business Machines
Bodie Marx, Mindscape, Inc.
Kenton Pattie, International Communications Industries Assn.
Carol Risher, American Association of Publishers
Linda Roberts, US Congress, Office of Technology Assessment
Donald A. Ross, Microcomputer Workshops Courseware
Lary Smith, Wayne Coiunty Intermediate School. Dist., Michigan
Ken Wasch, Software Publishers Association

For more information write to the ICCE Software Copyright Committee ICCE, University of Oregon, 1787 Agate St., Eugene, OR 97403

REFERENCES

The documents in this booklet were reproduced from the following sources:

"Agreement on Guidelines for Classroom Copying in Not-for-Profit Educational Institutions," U.S. House of Representatives, *Report No. 94-146,* Sect. 107.

"Guidelines for Educational Uses of Music," Ibid.

"Guidelines for Off-Air Recording of Broadcast Programming for Educational Purposes," *Congressional Record,* Oct. 14, 1981, p. E4751.

"Guidelines for Videotaping and Captioning Television Programs for Deaf and Hearing-impaired Students," *Congressional Record,* September 22, 1976, p. H10875.

"1987 Statement on Software Copyright: An ICCE Policy Statement" *The Computing Teacher,* March, 1987, pp. 52-53.

NEED MORE COPIES OF THIS BOOK?

01 to 10 copies $5.95 each
11 to 25 copies $4.25 each
26 to 50 copies $3.25 each
51 to 75 copies $2.25 each
76 or more $1.75 each

Shipping and handling charges will be added to reflect 4th class postage. Special handling requires additional fees. Payment must be made in U.S. dollars only. No telephone orders, please. Allow 4-6 weeks for delivery. Send your order to:

COPYRIGHT INFORMATION SERVICES
AECT Publication Sales
1025 Vermont Ave., NW, Suite 820
Washington, DC 20005

Other Titles Available from Copyright Information Services

COPYRIGHT POLICY DEVELOPMENT: A RESOURCE BOOK FOR EDUCATORS, Vlcek, Charles W. 1987, 165 pp....$37.95

Designed to help schools and colleges develop copyright policies that will help them observe the copyright laws. Includes many examples.

HIGH-TECH LAW (IN PLAIN ENGLISH(R): AN ENTREPRENEUR'S GUII DuBoff, Leonard D. 1991, 240 pp....$43.00

Useful for anyone planning a high-tech venture or a technology-related busine this book explains it all from venture capital to doing business overseas.

OFF-AIR VIDEOTAPING IN EDUCATION: COPYRIGHT ISSUES, DECISIONS, IMPLICATIONS, Sinofsky, Esther R. 1984, 163 pp....$34.95

Comprehensive treatment of the legal issues in videotaping off-the-air for classroom use. Included are seven appendices, plus three bibliographies and a index.

THE COPYRIGHT DIRECTORY: 1990-91, Miller, Jerome K. 134 pp....$99.9

This comprehensive directory lists all the key players in the copyright field. I the "Who's Who" of the copyright industry.

USING COPYRIGHTED VIDEOCASSETTES IN CLASSROOMS, LIBRARIES, AND TRAINING CENTERS, 2ND ED., Miller, Jerome K. 198 128 pp....$37.95

A thorough coverage of the legal requirements for showing videocassettes in schools, libraries, business, churches, etc.

VIDEO COPYRIGHT GUIDELINES FOR PASTORS & CHURCH WORKE Miller, Jerome K. 1986, 12 pp....$7.50

Guidelines for showing videocassettes in churches and church meeting rooms Prepared in conjunction with the National Council of Churches.

VIDEO COPYRIGHT PERMISSIONS: A GUIDE, Miller, Jerome K. 1989, pp....$44.95

Explains securing permissions from producers to use programs videotaped off the-air. Treats closed-circuit and satellite licenses.

Discounts available to bookstores and AECT members.